The Effective Teacher

A Christian's Guide to Teaching

Bennie E. Goodwin II

InterVarsity Press
DOWNERS GROVE, ILLINOIS 60515

© *1985 by Inter-Varsity Christian Fellowship of the United States of America*

All rights reserved. No part of this book may be reproduced in any form without written permission from InterVarsity Press, Downers Grove, Illinois.

InterVarsity Press is the book-publishing division of Inter-Varsity Christian Fellowship, a student movement active on campus at hundreds of universities, colleges and schools of nursing. For information about local and regional activities, write IVCF, 233 Langdon St., Madison, WI 53703.

Distributed in Canada through InterVarsity Press, 860 Denison St., Unit 3, Markham, Ontario L3R 4H1, Canada.

ISBN 0-87784-333-3

Printed in the United States of America

Library of Congress Cataloging in Publication Data
Goodwin, Bennie E., 1933-
  The effective teacher.

  Bibliography: p.
   1. Sunday-school teachers.   2. Christian education.
I. Title.
BV1534.G59   1985   268'.4   84-28869
ISBN 0-87784-333-3

15	14	13	12	11	10	9	8	7	6	5	4	3	2	1
96	95	94	93	92	91	90	89	88	87	86	85			

*Dedicated to
my mother
Odessa Christopher Goodwin
1908-1983
my first and dearest teacher*

Introduction	7
1 The Effective Teacher	*11*
2 Saved	*19*
3 Studious and Skilled	*25*
4 Spirit-Filled	*34*
5 Apples for the Teacher	*42*
Notes	*46*
Bibliography	*48*

INTRODUCTION

How wonderful it is to be a teacher. To be able to share with other persons an idea or skill is an exciting gift of God. And to be able to share that idea or skill in such a way that other persons can make it their own is even more exciting.

The gift of teaching seems to be universal. Every normal person teaches something to somebody somewhere at sometime. Can you think of a normal adult who doesn't fit that description? Mothers and fathers teach. Preachers and missionaries, doctors and lawyers teach. Musicians and secretaries, bus drivers and waitresses, scientists and politicians also teach, as do chemists and nurses, plumbers and electricians. Almost everybody teaches something to somebody somewhere at sometime.

Teaching is a wonderful, exciting gift of God. The purpose of this book is to talk about how we can use this gift effectively.

In the introduction to *The Effective Leader* we began with five basic assumptions.[1] They were:

1. Every normal person can lead.
2. Potential leaders are born, but effective leaders are made.
3. Effective leaders are the result of opportunity, training and experience.
4. The only way to learn to lead is to lead.
5. All normal Christians are expected to lead in the area of their gifts, talents and skills.

I believe these five assumptions are also true for teaching. Not only does every normal person have the capacity to teach, but every normal person can teach effectively.

Potential teachers, like leaders, are born. But effective teachers are made. Since almost everybody teaches something to somebody somewhere at sometime, it can be said that in a sense all normal persons are born teachers. But experience shows that effective teachers are rare, the result of a process that develops their God-given teaching capacity.

Effective teachers are the result of opportunity, training and experience. Given these three assets, we cannot expect every normal person to become a Confucius, a Buddha, a Socrates or an apostle Paul. But with these three assets, any normal high-school student, choir member or parent can effectively communicate their ideas and skills.

The only way to become an effective teacher, however, is to teach. Perhaps the most well-known American teacher-educator was John Dewey (1859-1952). "We learn by doing," is one of the slogans for which he is most well known. As most slogans, this one cannot stand by itself, nor is it true in every case. For instance, there are some truths better learned by listening and observation. It is better *not* to learn about the evils of alcoholism or narcotics addiction by personal experience. Such lessons are best learned from the warnings of Scripture or by observing other victims.

I'm sure Dewey was aware that learning by doing is not the only way to learn and that experience is not always the best teacher. But if a person is to become an effective teacher, experience is one of the indispensable components. Without actual practice, effective teaching is impossible.

Finally, I believe that every normal Christian is expected to teach. A Christian is one who follows Jesus Christ. Jesus is our Savior and Lord, but he is also known and universally accepted as the world's greatest teacher. In Matthew 9:35 we find one of the best summaries of his human activities: "Jesus went about all the cities and villages, teaching in their synagogues and preaching the gospel of the kingdom, and healing every disease and every infirmity."

As Jesus was about to leave his disciples, he told them to go into all the world and do four things: teach, preach, baptize and train converts to be disciples (Mt 28:19-20; Mk 16:15).

In light of the fact that Jesus was a master teacher and that he told his disciples to be teachers, I don't think it is stretching the point too far to say that the Lord *expects* all of his followers to be teachers. As Christ's disciples, we are *required* to teach.

Can we also say that he expects us not just to teach but to teach *effectively*—to develop knowledge, skill and character so that we can do our best and be our best for the glory of God and the good of others? If you believe that the Lord requires us to teach and your desire is to do God's will in this area of your life, then this book is for you. It is written to help you achieve that goal.

It is true that the only way to learn to teach is by actually teaching. So the purpose of this book is to suggest some *principles, techniques* and *perspectives* that will make the practice of teaching more purposeful, pleasant and productive.

1
THE EFFECTIVE TEACHER

You probably would have enjoyed knowing Socrates. He was a famous Greek philosopher and teacher who lived about four hundred years before Christ. One of the things that made him so interesting was his questions. He did not do a lot of lecturing to his students, but is famous for the dialogs or discussions which he often began with a two-word question, "To ti?" or "What is it?"

In this chapter we want to follow Socrates' example and look at three questions that are basic to our understanding of effective teaching: (1) What is teaching? (2) What is effective teaching? and (3) Who is an effective Christian teacher?

What Is Teaching?
Teaching is the science and art of communicating ideas and skills. What is happening when a mother is showing her child how to tie his shoe? She's teaching! What is taking place when a mother bird is showing a baby bird how to fly?

She's teaching! What is the activity called when a Sunday-school teacher is dramatizing for his class the reality of God's love? He's teaching! Teaching is the science and art of communicating ideas and skills.

Teaching is a science. Since some form of teaching exists in all known cultures, we can assume that some level of serious thought has been given to the principles of teaching throughout most of human history.[2]

We know, for instance, that Confucius in ancient China and Socrates, Plato and Aristotle among the Greeks considered teaching very important and are known today as four of history's great teachers. Among the Romans, the names of Cicero and Quintilian stand out, and Clement, Origen and Bede were outstanding pedagogical thinkers among the early church fathers.[3]

However, teaching as a science received its highest development during the eighteenth and nineteenth centuries. During that time such persons as Johann Pestalozzi (1746-1827), Johann Herbart (1776-1841) and Friedrich Froebel (1782-1852), did their work. They were followed by other educational luminaries—Horace Mann (1796-1859), Henry Barnard (1811-1900), Booker T. Washington (1856-1915), Maria Montessori (1870-1952) and John Dewey (1859-1952).[4]

Because of the thought and work of these persons and many others, teaching has developed into a recognized and honored profession. The teaching profession has an important history and a significant body of literature. Using knowledge gained from such disciplines as theology, philosophy, psychology and sociology, scholars have developed some generally agreed-upon principles about how, when, where and why learning and teaching best take place.

Dr. Milton Gregory's *Seven Laws of Teaching* offers a clear set of teaching principles. They are easy to remember and work well in actual teaching experiences.[5]

1. The law of the teacher: The teacher must know that which she or he would teach.
2. The law of the pupil: The pupil must attend with interest to the material being taught.
3. The law of the language: The language used in teaching must be common to the teacher and pupil.
4. The law of the lesson: The truth to be taught must be learned through truth already known.
5. The law of the teaching process: The teacher must direct the self-activities of the pupils and, as a rule, tell them nothing that they can learn for themselves.
6. The law of the learning process: The pupil must reproduce in his own mind the truth to be learned.
7. The law of review and application: The completion, test and confirmation of the work of teaching must be made by review and application.

These laws are scientific because they are universal and if diligently learned and properly applied will help any person applying them to be effective in teaching.

Teaching is an art. The art of teaching happens when individual teachers, consciously or unconsciously, apply these laws of teaching to their own teaching task in their own unique way. No two teachers are exactly alike and therefore no two teachers communicate ideas and skills in the same way.

Two teachers may teach the story of David and Goliath. Both may have the rapt attention and enthusiastic participation of the students and yet achieve their teaching goals in two entirely different ways. One may use music, the other art; another teacher may use drama. Other possibilities are hand puppets, dramatic readings, filmstrips or a combination of various methods and materials.

The "science" aspect of teaching is foundational. It gives teaching its universal dependability. The "art" aspect gives teaching its unique excitement and inexhaustible variety. Teaching is both a science and an art.

Teaching is communicating. Communicating involves at least three components—a transmitter, a message and a receiver. In teaching it is generally understood that the teacher is the transmitter, the lesson is the message, and the student is the receiver. That is the general understanding. In the actual teaching process, things do not work out quite so neatly.

In fact, sometimes in an exciting teaching session, the student will become the transmitter, while the teacher becomes the receiver.[6] Or in some cases, and especially in Christian teaching, the teacher's character actually becomes the message. One of Jesus' most challenging teaching sessions climaxed when he disclosed to his students that he was both the object and subject of his lesson. "I am the bread of life," he told them. "Eat me and live."

Wow! That's dramatic teaching at its best. As you remember, most of his students got the message and walked out of class. The core class remained and Jesus moved on (Jn 6:24-71). As you can see, a positive response is not always the outcome of communicating effectively. But for teaching to take place, the communicative components must be present. Teaching cannot happen where either the transmitter, the message or the receiver is missing.

Teaching is communicating ideas and skills. Ideas and skills are the matter of teaching. Teachers communicate information and give instructions. They present ideas, concepts and theories. And they teach people skills such as reading, typing and playing the piano. Teaching involves telling what and demonstrating how. It is concerned with the mind and the senses, the head and the hand. Teaching is communicating ideas and skills.

What Is Effective Teaching?

Having looked at teaching as the science and art of communicating ideas and skills, what is it that makes teaching effective? Is it possible to know the principles of teaching, to add one's own unique ways of communicating the ideas and skills and still not be effective? Or is effectiveness in teaching primarily a matter of mixing the right ingredients in the right way?

Perhaps a guarded yes is the answer to both of those questions. But specifically I think we can say that effective teaching is the science and art of communicating the right ideas and skills to the right persons in the right ways at the right times and places.

Of course there are wide areas where judgment must be exercised regarding what is "right." Rightness cannot always be determined in advance but must sometimes be worked out in the teaching situation. Teaching effectively has to do not only with knowing what and knowing how but also knowing who, when, where and why—and applying this knowledge in scientific and artistic ways. Here we are thinking of teaching effectiveness as an *activity*.[7]

However, the activity is built on an *attitude*. Effective teaching is a moving target. It is not a place of destination but a milestone along the way. It is a goal that is always in the future. Progress toward the goal of effective teaching is the result of the persistent acquiring and applying of knowledge, skill and judgment.

Who Is an Effective Christian Teacher?

We have saved this question for last, not only because it is built on the other two definitions, but also because it is the primary subject of the rest of the book. I would like to suggest the following sentence as our working definition of an effective Christian teacher: An effective Christian teacher is a person who communicates ideas, skills and ideals to inform, instruct and inspire students to know, do and be their best. Figure 1 is a diagram of this definition.

The added dimensions of the Christian teacher's task are in the right-hand column of the diagram. They stand out like a red neon sign on a dark night. The parts of our definition in the right-hand column remind us that we are not only

An Effective Christian Teacher

What am I teaching?	Ideas	Skills	Ideals
Why am I teaching?	To Inform	To Instruct	To Inspire
What results do I expect?	Knowledge	Skill	Christian Character

Figure 1.

concerned about knowledge and skill but most crucially about character.

We do not only inform and instruct our students by using ideas and skills so that they may know and do. We also want to inspire them with Christian ideals so that they can develop Christian character. The goal of Christian teaching is to help our students to *be* like Jesus, to be conformed to the image of Christ (Eph 4:13).

This concern did not originate with us but was expressed by our Lord and Master. Jesus was interested in people's bodies, as he illustrated by feeding the five thousand and by healing many. He was interested in people's minds as shown in his encounter with Mr. Legion and others who were possessed by demons (Mk 5:1-20). But his primary concern was about people's spiritual conditions. He was not only concerned that they know and do but that they be.

This is the Christian teacher's primary concern, which means that the Christian teacher must not only possess knowledge, skill and judgment, but must be a person of strong, positive Christian character. This added dimension is critical to the Christian teacher's effectiveness.

Strong, positive Christian character begins with the new birth (Jn 3:3, 5), or what is described in other parts of the New Testament as being "saved." The experience, process and purpose of salvation is discussed in chapter two. In chapter three we talk about effectiveness in relation to study and skill, and in chapter four we look at the Holy Spirit who helps us to be effective by filling us with joy, truth, power and love. The book concludes by reviewing some of the rewards of teaching and by listing some resources for further study.

The ideas and ideals in this book are for all persons who teach or wish to teach. But the major focus is toward those who want to be effective as *Christian* teachers.

This book says by its size that it does not even pretend to be exhaustive. But if it stimulates the reader to a deeper desire for knowledge, skill and character, it will be successful.

2
SAVED

At midnight in Philippi, there was a tremendous earthquake, probably 8.6 on the Richter scale. It was such an earthquake that the jail doors were shook open and the chains on Paul's hands and feet were unloosed. It was such an earthquake that it disoriented the jailer. He thought the prisoners had escaped and so he started to commit suicide.

"No, we're all here," Paul said. "Don't hurt yourself."

The Roman jailer knew that if he had been treated the way that he had treated Paul and Silas, he would have escaped at the first possible chance. But even more remarkable, he had heard Paul and Silas singing and praying after being beaten and put in chains.

The jailer concluded that Paul and Silas had an added dimension in their lives that was missing in his.

He then asked, "What must I do to be saved?"

Paul said, "Believe in the Lord Jesus, and you will be saved, you and your household" (Acts 16:19-31).

Effective Christian teachers are saved teachers. In the

Christian context there are at least three aspects to salvation. First, there is the personal *experience* of being delivered from the penalty and power of sin. Second, there is the *process* of being delivered from the practice of various individual sins. Third, there is the *conviction* that we are delivered from sin for the purpose of serving God by ministering to people.

Saved from Sin: An Experience

"Being saved" is one of the many biblical phrases that describes an experience that leads to a new relationship between an individual and God. One of the meanings of being saved is that of being rescued or delivered from danger or death.

As a teen-ager I looked out the window one day to discover that my brother had fallen into the pond at the back of our house. I went running out the back door, jumped into the pond and dragged him to safety.

By God's grace I *saved* him from drowning. It was truly by God's grace, because Samuel had already gone down twice and I couldn't even swim.

That episode describes our situation as human beings. We're sinking in and being overcome by the weight of our wrongdoing. And try as we may, we can't swim out of it. We can't save ourselves. Death is our destiny. The penalty for our sin is eternal separation from God, the source of life (Rom 6:23).

So God sent Jesus to demonstrate his love and to announce our forgiveness. If we believe his message, confess our sins and accept his forgiveness, we are saved, rescued, delivered from the penalty and power of our sin (1 Jn 1:9).

There are many other phrases and pictures by which biblical writers seek to express the experience of salvation. But basically what we're talking about is a change in one's attitude toward God. The change is from negative to positive, from independence to dependence, from self-confidence to trust in God, from a hateful or indifferent attitude to one of love. Being saved means the person undergoes a change in position, purpose, perspective and personality so radical that Jesus describes the experience as being "born again" (Jn 3:3); and Paul describes the individual as a "new creature" or "new creation" (2 Cor 5:17).

The crucial point for us is that without this experience, a person, no matter how knowledgeable and skilled, cannot be effective as a *Christian* teacher. This experience is critical because the Christian teacher's task is not simply to teach about a subject, even if it is religion or Christianity or the Bible or the Christian life. A Christian teacher's ultimate aim is to lead students to experience a new life in Jesus Christ and to help them grow into mature Christian persons.

Now can a teacher really do that, if she or he does not know Jesus Christ as their Savior and Lord? Can a teacher teach French who knows only Russian? Can a teacher teach basketball who has never played basketball? Can a teacher teach swimming who has never been in the water? If I am to effectively teach Jesus Christ, I must know him as my

Savior and Lord. I must be saved from sin.

Saved from "Stuff": A Process

Being saved from the penalty and power of sin is only the initial step in salvation. It is like the wedding ceremony which celebrates the beginning of a marriage. Likewise, the experience of salvation is the beginning of our new relationship with God. We are now ready for salvation as process. Jesus Christ not only saves us from sin, he also saves us from individual sins or what I call "stuff."

Remember Simon of Samaria in Acts 8:5-24? He was saved from sin by grace through faith. The Bible says "he believed." But when he saw all the wonderful things the Lord was doing through Peter, he interpreted what he saw on the basis of his background in magic and sorcery. He thought Peter was working tricks and asked Peter to sell him the secrets of his tremendous performance.

Peter got really upset. In effect, he told Simon that he was full of stuff, to take his money and get lost!

I really thought Peter was a little hard on Brother Simon, seeing that less than three months earlier Peter was full of stuff himself—cutting and cursing and denying that he even knew who Jesus was (Mt 26:69-75; Jn 18:15-27).

But then we all understand both Simon and Peter, because all of us have some stuff in us. Sometimes it's pride or temper or selfishness or procrastination or materialism.

Whatever our stuff is, we have to keep surrendering ourselves and our stuff to the Lord. If we don't, it will get in the way of our effectiveness as teachers. It will pop up at the wrong time in the wrong place and mar our testimony or cloud our witness or contradict the very lesson that we're trying so hard to teach. To be effective teachers we must be continually in the process of being saved from stuff by confessing it and surrendering it to the Lord (Rom 12:1-2).

Saved for Service: Our Purpose

There is a third aspect of salvation that contributes to a teacher's effectiveness. It is salvation for service. Jesus kept trying to convince his disciples that they were servants (Mt 20:20-28). He had a hard time since they knew so well what being a servant meant. It meant coming out of the fields tired, weary and worn and first preparing and serving dinner to the boss who had been "cooling it" all day in the "big house." It meant being forced to carry the weapons for the oppressors who used them to keep you in your place of forced servitude (Mt 5:41). It meant working at banquets in which you could not participate and washing the dirty feet of folk who stepped on you (Jn 13:5-6). But more than that, it meant taking orders and carrying out decisions in which you had no voice or vote—decisions that you knew were often against your best interests. It meant being deprived of essential personhood and that your social status was that of a tool. It meant that your basic identity was as your master's servant—Mr. John's cook, butler, horseman or farm hand.

Although most of the disciples had been small independent businessmen, they understood what it meant to be a servant and wanted no part of it. They wanted Jesus to establish a kingdom where they could sit on his right and left side and be vice president and secretary of state (Mt 20:20-28).

Jesus said that one day that will be; but the way to build the kingdom is not by military conquest but by service. Military conquest, force, violence leave too much death, destruction, hatred, bitterness and lusting for revenge in their wake. But a kingdom built on service lays foundations of love and builds walls of trust, hope and good will.

Even in our secular society teachers are looked upon as public servants, and all of the great teachers of the world—people like Confucius, Buddha, Socrates, Augustine, Gandhi, Martin Luther King, Jr., and Jesus Christ himself—were servants of society and men of peace.[8]

No matter what secular teachers strive for, Christian teachers are challenged to remain servants. To be effective as Christians, we must consecrate ourselves to our students—always seeking what is best with them and for them. We must consecrate ourselves to our teaching task—always putting aside adequate time, energy and effort to achieve excellence (Phil 1:10). And we must consecrate ourselves to God—always seeking his will, guidance and approval.

Effective teachers understand that the call to be a servant is a call to greatness. What did Jesus say? "Let the person who would be great be servant of all." An effective teacher is saved—from sin, from stuff and for service.

To serve this present age,
My calling to fulfill.
O may I my powers engage
To do my master's will.[9]

3
STUDIOUS AND SKILLED

Probably the most quoted verse among Christian educators is the sentence Paul wrote in his second letter to Timothy. "Study," it says in the King James Version, "to shew thyself approved unto God, a workman that needeth not to be ashamed, rightly dividing the word of truth" (2:15). Although the Greek word translated "study" does not really mean study in an academic sense, it does carry with it the general meaning of our word "studious." The Greek word means "be diligent, be persistently serious about or give concentrated attention to the task of."

Studious

Of course these words describe what effective teachers do. One of the first things that effective teachers are serious about is the study of their subjects. For instance, effective Bible teachers know their Bible. They know their Bible because they have given special time to studying it. They study it systematically. They know that there is no substitute for a series of Bible courses at a good Bible institute, Bible school, college or seminary.

If they cannot take daytime courses in regular educational institutions, they go to evening schools, attend seminars, take home-study courses, read helpful books and study information available on phonograph records, filmstrips and cassettes. They go to all the extra trouble it takes to seek out information because they want to be effective. They want to know as much as they can about the subject they're teaching. They want to know such things as Bible history and geography, language and customs, instruments and tools, plants and animals. All of this information gives depth of understanding to the teacher which can be passed on at appropriate times in specific lessons.

Having done the basic foundational study of the subject, the effective teacher does not neglect the thorough study of the specific lesson under consideration. For instance, Sunday-school teachers should start at least a week early and read the specific passage to be taught every day. Besides getting intimately acquainted with the passage, they may discover new truths "popping up." New angles of approach and fresh perspectives on old words reveal themselves. As they read each day the excitement grows, new examples and applications emerge.

It's beautiful and amazing how a lesson can come alive as it becomes more familiar. Visual aids will come to mind. Ways of dramatizing the stories, object lessons, illustrations—all kinds of ways to express the exciting discoveries are born. You'll have to pick among the treasures and restrain yourself from trying to give too much. This kind of

STUDIOUS AND SKILLED

teaching is very exhilarating for the students and the teacher. Effective teachers are enthusiastic teachers. They know their lesson.

Another thing that makes teachers effective is that they *know their students*. They study their students. Take Brenda James for instance. She teaches teen-agers. She seems not to mind taking courses in adolescent psychology. She attends youth seminars, reads all kinds of books on dating, sex, drugs, careers and all the things that are teen-age preoccupations. She literally immerses herself in knowledge about teens.

And then she spends a lot of time with her class—talking with them and listening to them. She has them over to her house for parties and goes with them to their school honor days, award banquets, sports events and graduations. She has very few discipline problems in her class, attendance is consistently high, and many of her class go on to Christian colleges and into church-related careers.

Brenda is an effective teacher. She is a born-again Christian. She knows her subject, constantly studies her lessons and seeks to know her students at ever deeper levels. She prays for them daily and fellowships with them often. No wonder they're anxious to get to her class and reluctant to leave. Lord, give us more studious teachers like Brenda!

Whether the subject is science, philosophy, math, chemistry or tennis, effective teachers know their subjects because they are diligent in study. And whether the students are senior citizens or preschool children, we need to know them and love them if we are to do our best teaching. Opportunities and conditions are seldom ideal, but teachers who are determined to be effective accept their conditions, take advantage of their opportunities and with the Lord's help make the best of what is at hand.

Teaching that influences positive changes in students' lives is not easy. It costs the teacher extra time, effort, energy and money. But teachers who wish to do and be their best are willing to make such an investment.

Skilled

Let's take an imaginary trip to Sleepy Hollow Christian College (SHCC). First let's visit Dr. Boring's class. Now if there's anyone who should be effective, surely it should be Dr. Boring. He is a good Christian man, he has a wonderful family and is a trustee at Sleepy Hollow Evangelical Church. He has five degrees—a B.A. in religion and philosophy, three master's degrees in philosophy, archaeology and biblical languages, and a Ph.D. in Old Testament studies. The man is heavy! He knows his subject.

Then why do so many Bible majors dread going to his lectures? Why did so many students change their majors to sociology, Christian education and music when they came to SHCC all excited about studying the Scriptures?

Well, let's ask some of the students.

Interviewer (Int.): Mary, why did you change your major?
Mary: Well . . . really . . . I mean . . . Boring really lives up to his name.
Int.: You mean he's boring? Doesn't he know his

STUDIOUS AND SKILLED

	material?
Bob:	Yes. The man really knows his stuff. He not only has all these degrees but he's actually been to Jerusalem and many of the places he teaches about.
Int.:	Well, then why . . . .
Mary:	His problem is he knows *what* to teach but . . .
Julia:	But doesn't know *how* to teach.
Bob:	Yes, that's a major problem here at SHCC. We have some really well-educated teachers here, but it seems like they've never had any courses on how to teach.
Mary:	I mean, we had better teaching in high school.
Jim:	Yeah, the teachers used records and pictures . . .
Julia:	And films and object lessons . . .
Bob:	Dr. Boring must have taken some pictures during his time in Palestine.
Mary:	That would brighten up the class some . . .
Jim:	Even a little discussion or one or two student reports . . .
Julia:	Even some map work would help.
Mary:	I mean, this lecture, Lecture, LECTURE is driving me mad!

I think we all know how Mary feels. We've all had the Dr. Boring experience. Actually with a little thought and effort Dr. Boring could become a Dr. Interesting.

Dr. Interesting knows that there are keys to an interesting, exciting lesson. And the first key is the *enthusiasm of the teacher.* If the lesson is exciting to the teacher, it's hard for the students not to be interested.

The second key is *variety*. Each class should consist of three or four different learning activities. At a minimum, there should be looking, listening, talking and writing activities. And with young children, there should be some kind of physical movement also.

The third key to an interesting lesson is the *use of objects that appeal to the senses*. Dr. Interesting consistently brings in things for her students to see, to hear and to touch. Occasionally she comes to class with things to smell and taste. And if sense-objects are not available for a particular lesson, she will use sense-appeal words. She recognizes that these words do not adequately substitute for the real objects, but in various ways she tries to come as close as possible to the real things.

The fourth key to an interesting lesson is *participation*. We asked Dr. Interesting why she did so little lecturing. She said that besides boring the students, it did not give them a chance to discover things for themselves. She said, "I have a lot of class presentations. It makes the students do their reading and research, and gives them practice in standing before the class, presenting their material and expressing their ideas. After all, that's what most of them will be doing the rest of their lives. So in my class they get some good practice.

"And then too," she went on, "it adds interest to the class time. There are more voices heard in the room. Let's face it, one voice for an hour—even if it's my voice—is hard on the ears, not to mention having to look at the same face and the same clothes. Know what I mean?" Yes, Doc. I think we know what you mean. And we know why students call you "Dr. Interesting." We'll remember those keys to skill in effective teaching: enthusiasm, variety, sense appeal and participation.

Christian Teacher Skills

During our interviews, we asked the students at SHCC if there were other skills needed by Christian teachers to help them be effective. They suggested three other skills that were very important to them.

Bob, an Inter-Varsity Christian Fellowship officer and education major, said he thought every Christian teacher should be skilled in *leading students to Christ*. Mary and Jim agreed with Bob. They said that every teacher should know such key salvation verses as Matthew 1:21, John 1:11-12, 3:16-17, Acts 16:30-31, Romans 3:23, 6:23, 10:9-10 and Revelation 3:20.

Mary, who hopes to enter Meharry Medical School after college, emphasized that she meant *every* Christian teacher—whether teaching in a Sunday school, Bible club or university. She said she felt that it was a crucial skill for any Christian to possess, but that certainly any Christian teacher should be able to sense when a student is seeking Christ and be able through listening, encouragement, Scripture and prayer to lead that person to an experience of personal salvation.

Julia, a Sunday-school teacher at Zion Baptist, said that she had a special appreciation for teachers who possessed *counseling skills.* She thought that a course in Christian counseling would increase a teacher's effectiveness. But if not a course, at least reading or listening to some tapes by professional Christian counselors like Clyde Narramore, Lawrence Crabb or Everett Worthington would help.[10] In fact, she confided that most teachers just need to learn not to talk so much and to listen more patiently when their students come in to talk with them. She said sometimes students don't really want a lot of advice. They just want someone to listen to them and to pray with them. Other students and some professional counselors have made the same observations.

Jim, who wants to be a pastor, said Mr. Bill Ding really impressed him as an effective teacher because he kept telling his students that they were the church's future leaders.[11] Jim said, "Every time a prominent Christian leader came within a reasonable distance, Mr. Ding would invite him to our class and present him as a kind of model. He would have us write about such persons as D. L. Moody, Billy Graham, Martin Luther King, Jr., Mary Bethune and Francis Schaeffer. He would then have us share our research in class.

"He would assign us to go listen to outstanding preachers, teachers, administrators, writers, missionaries and musicians. After our visits we made reports to the class. He was forever reminding us of our leadership potentials and challenging us to develop them. He never got tired of quoting Matthew 9:35-38, especially the part 'the harvest is plentiful, but the laborers are few.' And by the end of a semester in his class, you felt like your life was an important gift from God and that you owed it to him to make a significant contribution to the work of the kingdom. As a teacher, Mr. Ding was quite effective in helping to make leaders out of us."

In addition to being skilled communicators—knowing how to teach as well as what to teach—Christian teachers add to their effectiveness by knowing how to lead students to Christ, how to counsel and how to inspire students toward Christian leadership.

4
SPIRIT-FILLED

Besides being saved, studious and skilled, a fourth characteristic of an effective teacher is being Spirit-filled.[12] "But what exactly does it mean to be Spirit-filled?" That was the question Barbara Thomas raised. Barbara is a bright, vibrantly alive primary teacher at the East End Presbyterian Church. She's also a professional teacher and both her Sunday-school and public school students love her. She is a committed Christian and ardent church worker. But she is mystified by all the talk about being Spirit-filled. The more she heard about the Holy Spirit and various people's spiritual experiences, the more confused she became. So one day she cornered her pastor, the Rev. Mr. C. J. Louis, and asked him pointblank, "What does it mean to be Spirit-filled?"

The Spirit-Filled Life

First, Pastor Louis assured her that *being Spirit-filled is biblical.* It is not a new fad thought up by Pentecostals or charismatics, but the phrase itself is scriptural. They then went into Pastor Louis's study and looked up such Scriptures as Luke 1:15, 67; Acts 2:1-11; 10:44-46 and Ephesians 5:18-20. Sister Barbara discovered that all of these passages and many more speak of being filled with the Spirit.

Second, Pastor Louis pointed out that *the Spirit is God.* They turned to John 4:24 where Jesus tells the woman at the well that "God is Spirit." They looked at other Bible verses such as Genesis 1:2-5 where it becomes clear that God not only exists as a divine Person, but is active in his universe.

To Barbara's question about why he is called the *Holy* Spirit, Pastor Louis said that the word *holy* distinguishes God as Spirit from human spirits and from evil spirits.

The third thing that Pastor Louis pointed out to Barbara was that since the Spirit is God and God is a person, being filled with the Spirit is not like a bottle being filled with water. It is not having an amount of something but *having a relationship* with Someone. God is that Someone and the basis of that relationship is love.

God loves us—always has and always will. The more we love him, the more our lives are influenced by him; so that our purposes, perspectives, desires and activities are more and more determined by his purposes, perspectives, desires and activities. The more intimate our relationship with him becomes, the more our thoughts, time, money, ambitions, hopes and dreams are determined by what he says is best for us. Our whole personality—mind, body, soul and spirit—is saying yes to all that we understand God's love requires.

For some people, becoming Spirit-filled is an experience that occurs all at once—like when two people in love commit their lives to each other in marriage. The emotions experienced at the moment of saying yes to God are expressed in various ways depending on the person, the circumstances and what God is seeking to accomplish. For example, compare Jesus' experience in Matthew 3:16-17 with the disciples' experience in Acts 2:1-11 and Paul's experience in Acts 9:17-18. Each expression of the spiritual experience is different.[13] Many may find that being Spirit-filled is more of a slow growth than a momentary experience.

But whichever is the case, being filled with the Spirit is a process. It is a process of growth and development. It is a process of maturing in our relationship to God through Jesus Christ. It is becoming more and more like Jesus, our ultimate spiritual model (Eph 4:14-16). It is asking and allowing the Spirit—through prayer, the Scriptures, worship, fellowship and service—to produce in our lives the spiritual qualities found in Galatians 5:22-23: the gifts of love, peace, patience and so on. The more this growing process takes place, the more fully we are controlled by the Spirit, and the more effective we become as Christian teachers or whatever ministry to which the Lord has called us.

Characteristics of a Spirit-Filled Person

Later Sister Barbara shared what she had learned about the Holy Spirit with James Lawson, the Christian education director. Together they came up with the idea of inviting Pastor Louis to the next Christian education department meeting. He came and shared with the teachers and

SPIRIT-FILLED 37

Christian education workers what he and Sister Barbara had discussed. During the presentation, Melba Jean asked him to describe the characteristics of a Spirit-filled teacher.

First, he said that a Spirit-controlled teacher is a *thankful* teacher (Eph 5:18-20). Renee Johnson pointed out that joy is one of the first personality characteristics that the Spirit develops in a person's life (Gal 5:22-23). And June Thomas observed that Jesus was a thankful person (Mt 26:27; Jn 6:11; 11:41) and that the day of Pentecost was a very joyous occasion (Acts 2:1-21). The reading of other Scriptures such as Philippians 4:4, Colossians 3:16-17 and 1 Thessalonians 5:16-18 convinced everybody that a Spirit-filled teacher is a thankful teacher. And that a happy, joyful teacher is actually a more effective one.

A second group of Scripture passages show that the Holy Spirit is the "Spirit of truth" (Jn 14:16-17; 15:26; 16:7-14). Brother Larry Alexander, a teacher of junior boys and a campus staff worker at Louisiana State University, observed that the Holy Spirit is also called the Spirit of Christ. And Christ, he said, always told the truth. Therefore if a person is fully controlled by Christ's Spirit, telling the truth and being truthful ought to be a logical outcome. Brenda cited other Scriptures such as Ephesians 4:15, 25; 6:14. There was really little discussion on this point. Everybody generally agreed that it is a contradiction in terms for one who is not consistently truthful in word and deed to claim to be controlled by the Spirit of truth. A Spirit-filled teacher is a *truthful* teacher.

A third group of Scripture passages speaks of the power

of the Holy Spirit. In Acts 1:8 Jesus told his disciples that they would receive power after the Holy Spirit came upon them, Brother Larry pointed out that the power is for worldwide evangelism. But June Thomas said that according to Matthew 28:18-20, the power was for teaching. All the teachers chimed in their agreement.

Pastor Louis said that the power was available to make believers productive. So that whatever assignment God gives believers, the Holy Spirit empowers them to do their task.

Various other members cited passages such as Acts 6:1-6, where the Spirit gave power to make decisions and to do miracles; and 1 Corinthians 12:1-3, where the Spirit gave power to confess Jesus as Lord. Everybody agreed that the Spirit-filled teacher is a *Spirit-empowered* teacher.

Pastor Louis wrapped up the session by asking everybody to write down a word that more than any other described the indispensable characteristic of a Spirit-filled believer. The response was unanimous. The word was *love*.

After briefly looking at such verses as John 13:1, 34-35; Acts 2:44-47 and Galatians 5:22, Pastor Louis was almost ready to pray the closing prayer when June sighed despairingly, "The Spirit-filled teacher is perfect. I'll never make it!"

"Not really," Pastor Louis responded. "There is usually some part of our personality that is rebelling against total Spirit-control. Complete Spirit-control is more of a goal than an achievement."

Brother Larry gave the example from his days in military service. "Sometimes," he said, "the center city of our personalities has surrendered to the Spirit's control, but there always seems to be an outlying village that remains a guerilla stronghold."

Brenda said, "Then Spirit-control is not so much an experience as it is a process."

"According to Scripture," said Pastor Louis, "it is both. There are specific times when we consciously say, 'Yes, Lord, have your way. I surrender to your will.' And it is at those times that we experience a tremendous infusion of the Spirit's joy, power and love. But in the process of our spiritual growth we have many of these times. As we come to know the Lord and to know ourselves, we realize that our spiritual lives are punctuated by commas, dashes and colons but seldom are there any periods. The Spirit-filled life is one of thanks, truth, power and love. It is a life of growth. The more we become like Jesus, the better we understand how much unlike him we still are. So that a Spirit-filled person is also characterized by humility and patience, as well as all of those other qualities found in Galatians 5:22-23."

Everybody nodded and said "Amen" and the session came to an end with prayer and the reading of 1 Corinthians 13.

Each person went home a little more aware of the Spirit's presence and his desire to make them more thankful, truthful, empowered and loving teachers.

Being filled with the Holy Spirit is important to us as teachers because we cannot be our most effective without him. We are called upon to influence our students' characters, but the fact is we cannot even effect changes in our own character. Our task is to help victims of hatred to be loving, to help victims of oppression to be liberators, to help victims of doubt to be faith-full and victims of despair to be full of hope. We can't do it—not by ourselves. We need the Holy Spirit.

We can teach the what and how, the knowledge and skills, but effective Christian teaching is more than that. It is about radical, positive personality change. It is about making people new. It is about producing kingdom people. It is about influencing and equipping persons whom God can use as he did Moses and David, Peter and Paul, Augustine and Luther, John Wesley and Richard Allen, Charles Harrison Mason and Benjamin Mays. To accomplish our task we need more than knowledge and skill, we need more than the best we can be. We need the truth, the love and the power of God revealed to us through Jesus Christ and made available to us by the Holy Spirit.

Over two billion people go to bed hungry every night. There are ten million alcoholics in our country and a serious crime is committed every three seconds. Since 1900 almost one hundred million people have been killed in war.

After nearly two thousand years of Christian witness, there are still over three billion people who don't know Christ as their Savior. Christian teachers have a job to do. I know we can't solve all of the world's problems alone, but we must do all we can. We must use all of our knowledge and skills; we must know our subjects and our students. We must do our best to prepare our heads and hands to perform our professional tasks. But we must do more. We must make sure that we are thoroughly Christian in attributes, attitudes and actions. We must make ourselves fully available to God so that his Spirit can flow into us and through us to do his will and to accomplish his purposes in the world.

Our names will probably not appear in the morning paper, on the movie marquee or on the six o'clock news. We will probably not be the subject of books on great Christians. We may die relatively anonymous and unheralded. But we are the persons who must prepare the persons who stand in the spotlight. What we allow the Holy Spirit to do to us and through us with our students in and outside of our classrooms will determine much of the effectiveness of the next generation's Christian leadership. And so we pray with the poet George Croly:

Spirit of God, descend upon my heart;
Wean it from earth, through all its pulses move;
Stoop to my weakness, mighty as Thou art,
And make me love Thee as I ought to love. . . .
Teach me to love Thee as Thine angels love,
One holy passion filling all my frame;
The baptism of the heaven-descended Dove,
My heart an altar, and Thy love the flame.

5
APPLES FOR THE TEACHER

Teaching is challenging but there are rewards. There is the *personal reward* of doing something well. Jesus told a story in which the first words of commendation were "well done" (Lk 19:11-27). In a sense, being a good teacher, just as being a good preacher, doctor, artist or secretary, is its own reward. The deep feeling of satisfaction that comes from having prepared oneself and completed a worthwhile task is itself a wonderful prize. To know that we have done well and been good and faithful teachers is one of life's greatest rewards.

Second, there is the *professional reward*. There is a special sense of achievement that a teacher feels on promotion day or at the graduation ceremonies as the students march across the stage to receive their certificates. Knowing that their knowledge has been increased, some of their skills developed, their talents discovered and their spiritual sensitivities heightened—that is reward.

And then the day comes when they return to say "thank

you." They are taller now, more poised and mature with a greater sense of purpose and direction. And they have begun to recognize the part you played in their development. They stand at your desk, smiling down on you, expressing their gratitude—there is no day like that day in the life of a teacher. It is one of the great rewards of the profession.

A third kind of reward might be called *social*. While it is true that very few of the "old" professions inspire the same awe as in days gone by, the society and the church still hold effective teachers in generally high regard. And in spite of television, computers, programmed learning and robots, there is no replacement for the effective teacher in the foreseeable future. This is true in the society-at-large and especially true in our churches and church-related educational institutions. I suppose we might also think of this reward as job security, since, as a professional group, effective teachers are still indispensable.

You have probably noticed that we have not listed "finances" as one of the rewards for effective teaching. That omission is deliberate. Even effective professional teachers usually do not receive pay commensurate with their educational preparation and general influence. There are exceptions, but even those teachers who receive above-average pay are usually not paid what their counterparts are paid in professions like law, medicine and engineering.

However, we receive some rewards that help equalize the difference. With the exception of certain inner-city situations, teaching is a relatively low-risk occupation. The stress level is lower and the general life expectancy is longer than many higher paying professions.

A teacher is expected to live a relatively simple life and except for educational expenses, there are usually no great personal outlays of money for equipment and materials. Teachers have the privilege of indulging in the life of the mind and spirit. And of course one really wonderful reward is the long summer vacation.

However, the teacher's greatest rewards are *spiritual*. An effective Christian teacher is constantly challenged to grow in spiritual awareness and availability to God. This is an absolute necessity if one is to be effective. But it is also a wonderful reward to see one's spiritual life develop deeper, wider and higher dimensions.

Another spiritual reward is to see the influence of the Spirit in the lives of others. To watch the Lord use our words and deeds to affect the personalities and situations of those around us is an inspiring spiritual experience. To see others develop a greater spiritual consciousness, to see their attitudes become more positive, to see an enlivened interest in church attendance and participation, to see the exercise of more love, patience and understanding in interpersonal relationships, to see a professed or practical atheist admit to spiritual emptiness, become repentant for past sins and turn to Christ—these are spiritual rewards. To watch students accept Jesus Christ as their Savior and to see them grow in the Lord to the point where they become positive Christian influences in the lives of others is our highest reward.

Ultimately our reward is to do as Jesus did: to make disciples who will make disciples who will make disciples—

to drop tiny pebbles of God's Word into the vast ocean of time until the ripples touch the shores of eternity.

In this way, the timely becomes timeless and the teacher's mortal life becomes immortal.

> A Builder built a temple,
> He wrought it with grace and skill;
> Pillars and groins and arches
> All fashioned to work his will.
> Men said, as they saw its beauty,
> "It shall never know decay;
> Great is thy skill, O Builder!
> Thy fame shall endure for aye."
>
> A Teacher built a temple
> With loving and infinite care,
> Planning each arch with patience,
> Laying each stone with prayer.
> None praised her unceasing efforts,
> None knew of her wondrous plan,
> For the temple the Teacher builded
> Was unseen by the eyes of man.
>
> Gone is the Builder's temple,
> Crumpled into dust;
> Low lies each stately pillar,
> Food for consuming rust.
> But the temple the Teacher builded
> Will last while the ages roll,
> For that beautiful unseen temple
> Was a child's immortal soul.[14]

Notes

[1] Bennie Goodwin, *The Effective Leader* (Downers Grove, Ill.: InterVarsity Press, 1981), pp. 7-10.

[2] See Elmer Wilds and Kenneth Lottich, *Foundations of Modern Education* (New York: Holt, Rinehart and Winston, 1965).

[3] See Robert Ulich, *History of Educational Thought* (New York: American Book Company, 1950). See also William Maxwell et al., *The Philosophy and History of Education* (New York: Monarch Press, 1963), pp. 5-21. Also Betty Kelen, *Confucius: In Life and Legend* (New York: Nelson, 1972).

[4] Merritt Thompson, *The History of Education* (New York: Barnes and Noble, 1961), pp. 42-52.

[5] Milton Gregory, *Seven Laws of Teaching* (Grand Rapids, Mich.: Baker, 1975). For a very brief restatement of the laws with commentary in outline form, see Bennie Goodwin, ed., *Steps to Dynamic Teaching* (Atlanta: Goodpatrick, 1980).

[6] For a fuller exposition of this concept, see Paulo Freire, *Pedagogy of the Oppressed,* trans. by Myra Ramos (New York: Seabury Press, 1973). For a summary of Freire's educational philosophy, see Bennie Goodwin's "Paulo Freire: Educator for Liberation," in *Reflections on Education* (Atlanta: Goodpatrick, 1978), pp. 67-92.

[7] For a discussion of education as an activity, see J. Gordon Chamberlin, *Toward a Phenomenology of Education* (Philadelphia: Westminster, 1969), pp. 9-10.

[8] Mohandas Gandhi and Martin Luther King, Jr., are not usually thought of as teachers. For a fuller exposition of this idea, see D. B. Norman,

Fourteen Great Thinkers (Atlanta: Goodpatrick, 1979), pp. 40-46; also Goodwin, *Reflections on Education,* pp. 19-66.

[9] From Charles Wesley's hymn "A Charge to Keep I Have."

[10] Clyde Narramore, *The Psychology of Counseling* (Grand Rapids, Mich.: Zondervan, 1960). See also Lawrence Crabb, *Basic Principles of Biblical Counseling* (Grand Rapids, Mich.: Zondervan, 1975).

[11] See Kenneth Gangel, *Building Leaders for Church Education* (Chicago: Moody, 1981); Ted Engstrom, *The Making of a Christian Leader* (Grand Rapids, Mich.: Zondervan, 1976); and John Alexander, *Managing Your Work* (Downers Grove, Ill.: InterVarsity Press, 1975).

[12] For an extensive discussion of the Holy Spirit, see Hendrikus Berkhof, *The Doctrine of the Holy Spirit* (Atlanta: Knox, 1982).

[13] For some further thought on the relationship between religious experience and religious expression, see Howard Thurman, *The Search for Common Ground* (New York: Harper and Row, 1971). For a brief discussion of the relationship between religious experience, expression, and environment, see Bennie Goodwin, ed., *Six Major Religions* (Atlanta: Goodpatrick, 1978), pp. 5-6.

[14] Anonymous, "The Builder."

Bibliography

Boehlke, Robert. *Theories of Learning in Christian Education*. Philadelphia: Westminster, 1962.

Bowman, Locke. *Teaching Today: The Church's First Ministry*. Philadelphia: Westminster, 1980.

Chamberlin, J. Gordon. *Toward a Phenomenology of Education*. Philadelphia: Westminster, 1969.

Eavey, C. B. *Principles of Teaching*. Grand Rapids, Mich.: Zondervan, 1968.

Freire, Paulo. *Pedagogy of the Oppressed*. Translated by Myra Ramos. New York: Seabury Press, 1973.

Gangel, Kenneth. *Building Church Leaders for Church Education*. Chicago: Moody, 1981.

Goodwin, Bennie. *Reflections on Education*. Atlanta: Goodpatrick, 1978.

——————. *Steps to Dynamic Teaching*. Atlanta: Goodpatrick, 1980.

——————. *The Effective Leader*. Downers Grove, Ill.: InterVarsity Press, 1981.

Gregory, Milton. *Seven Laws of Teaching*. Grand Rapids, Mich.: Baker, 1975.

Norman, D. B. *Fourteen Great Thinkers*. Atlanta: Goodpatrick, 1979.

Rogers, Donald. *In Praise of Learning*. Nashville: Abingdon, 1980.

Wynn, J. C. *Christian Education for Liberation*. Nashville: Abingdon, 1977.